At Sylvan, we believe reading is one of life's most important and enriching abilities, and we're glad you've chosen our resources to help your child build these critically important skills. We know that the time you spend with your child reinforcing the lessons learned in school will contribute to his love of reading. This love of reading will translate into academic achievement. A successful reader is ready for the world around him, ready to do research, ready to experience the world of literature, and prepared to make the connections necessary to achieve in school and in life.

We use a research-based, step-by-step process in teaching reading at Sylvan that includes thought-provoking reading selections and activities. As students increase their success as readers they become more confident. With increasing confidence, students build even more success. Our Sylvan workbooks are designed to help you to help your child build the skills and confidence that will contribute to your child's success in school.

We're excited to partner with you to support the development of a confident, well-prepared independent learner!

The Sylvan Team

Sylvan Learning Center.
Unleash your child's potential here.

No matter how big or small the academic challenge, every child has the ability to learn. But sometimes children need help making it happen. Sylvan believes every child has the potential to do great things. And we know better than anyone else how to tap into that academic potential so that a child's future really is full of possibilities. Sylvan Learning Center is the place where your child can build and master the learning skills needed to succeed and unlock the potential you know is there.

The proven, personalized approach of our in-center programs deliver unparalleled results that other supplemental education services simply can't match. Your child's achievements will be seen not only in test scores and report cards but outside the classroom as well. And when he starts achieving his full potential, everyone will know it. You will see a new level of confidence come through in everything he does and every interaction he has.

How can Sylvan's personalized in-center approach help your child unleash his potential?

• Starting with our exclusive Sylvan Skills Assessment®, we pinpoint your child's exact academic needs.

• Then we develop a customized learning plan designed to achieve your child's academic goals.

• Through our method of skill mastery, your child will not only learn and master every skill in his personalized plan, he will be truly motivated and inspired to achieve his full potential.

To get started, simply contact your local Sylvan Learning Center to set up an appointment. And to learn more about Sylvan and our innovative in-center programs, call 1-800-EDUCATE or visit www.SylvanLearning.com. *With over 750 locations in North America, there is a Sylvan Learning Center near you!*

Kindergarten
Beginning Word Games
Workbook

Published in the United States by Random House, Inc., New York, and in Canada by Random House of Canada Limited, Toronto.

This book was previously published with the title *Kindergarten Beginning Word Games* as a trade paperback by Sylvan Learning, Inc., an imprint of Penguin Random House LLC, in 2009.

www.sylvanlearning.com

Created by Smarterville Productions LLC
Producer: TJ Trochlil McGreevy
Producer & Editorial Direction: The Linguistic Edge
Writer: Erin Lassiter
Cover and Interior Illustrations: Duendes del Sur
Cover Design: Suzanne Lee
Layout and Art Direction: SunDried Penguin
Art Manager: Adina Ficano

First Edition

ISBN: 978-0-375-43021-3

Library of Congress Cataloging-in-Publication Data available upon request.

This book is available at special discounts for bulk purchases for sales promotions or premiums. For more information, write to Special Markets/Premium Sales, 1745 Broadway, MD 6-2, New York, New York 10019 or e-mail specialmarkets@randomhouse.com.

PRINTED IN CHINA

10 9 8 7 6

Contents

X Marks the Spot

LOOK at the words in the word box. Can you find these things in the **winter** picture?
PUT an X over each one.

snow	tree	owl	rock	fox	snowman

Mystery Picture

FIND the spaces with the word **fall**. COLOR those spaces red to see the mystery picture.

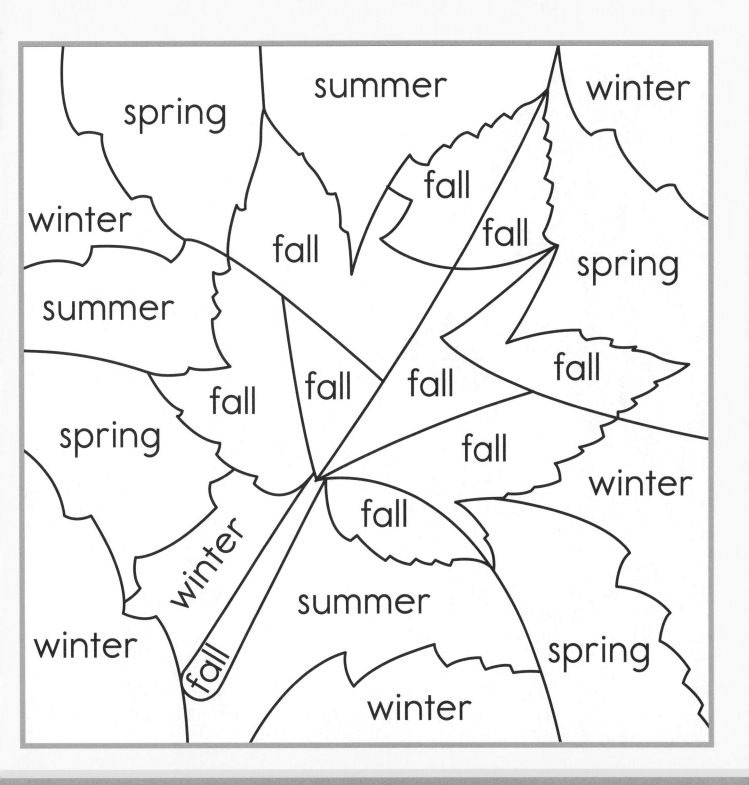

X Marks the Spot

LOOK at the words in the word box. Can you find these things in the **summer** picture? PUT an X over each one.

sun   ant   ball   bird   grass   dog

Mystery Picture

FIND the spaces with the word **spring**. COLOR those spaces pink to see the mystery picture.

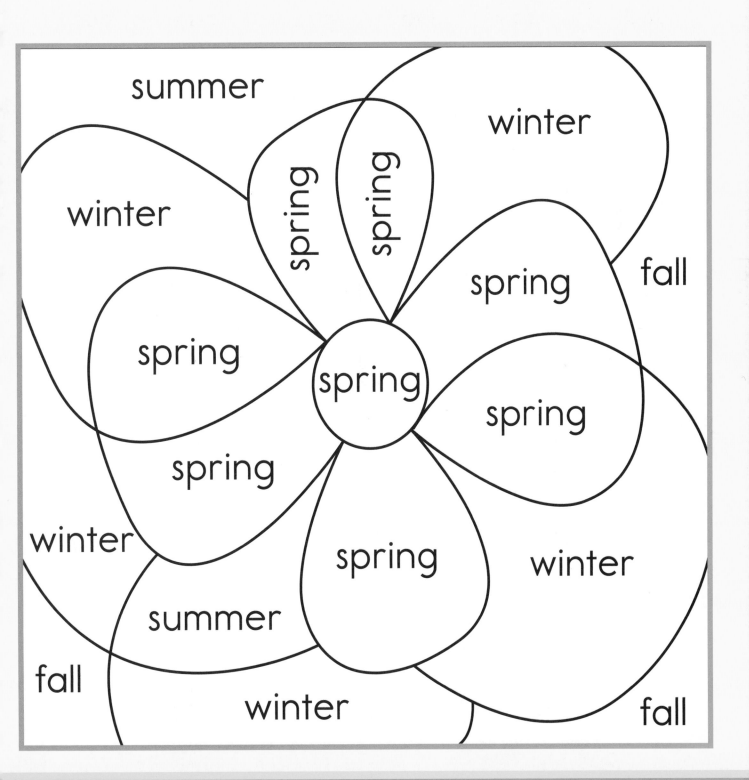

Word Hunt

CIRCLE the words in the grid that end in **-ad**.
Words go across and down.

| sad | bad | dad | had | mad | pad |

a	z	q	c	l	h	k
e	b	n	s	f	a	m
s	a	f	a	u	d	x
f	d	m	d	v	w	d
h	j	u	o	p	i	a
r	c	m	a	d	s	d
y	q	g	f	o	e	l
p	a	d	t	v	b	a

Pond Crossing

DRAW a line through the words that end in **-ad** to help the frog jump across the pond.

Start

mad · cat · rat · yam

sad · ham · ram · jam

hat

dam · pad · lad · mat

sat · dad

End

Word Hunt

-ag

CIRCLE the words in the grid that end in **-ag**.
Words go across and down.

| bag | rag | sag | tag | wag |

a	e	z	x	d	s	h
w	y	u	r	e	a	c
a	c	r	a	s	g	p
g	b	v	g	j	k	w
i	l	m	h	e	t	s
b	a	g	y	t	f	h
o	r	v	u	a	b	k
t	n	i	s	g	q	d

Find the Path

DRAW a line through the words that end in **-ag** to help the ant out of the anthill.

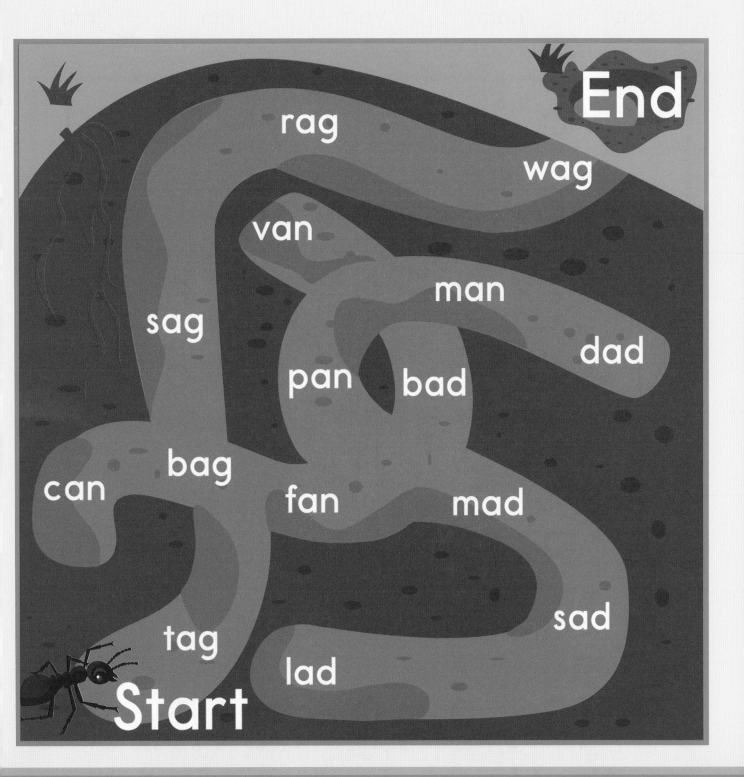

Word Hunt

CIRCLE the words in the grid that end in **-am**.
Words go across or down.

dam	ham	yam	ram	jam

h	a	m	e	y	b	d
c	k	m	i	a	r	p
q	z	x	o	m	n	e
u	d	a	m	v	o	j
r	t	s	h	f	i	a
j	q	c	u	l	s	m
r	a	m	r	e	w	z
a	g	p	o	t	t	e

Find the Path

DRAW a line through the words that end in **-am** to help the ram down the mountain.

Start

rag

ram

nag

wag

bag

dam

fat

yam

tag

rat

mat

pat

jam

End   ham   hat

Connect the Dots

DRAW a line to connect the words that sound like **mad**. Connect them in ABC order.

HINT: I sit in the sand under the sea. An ocean animal lives in me.

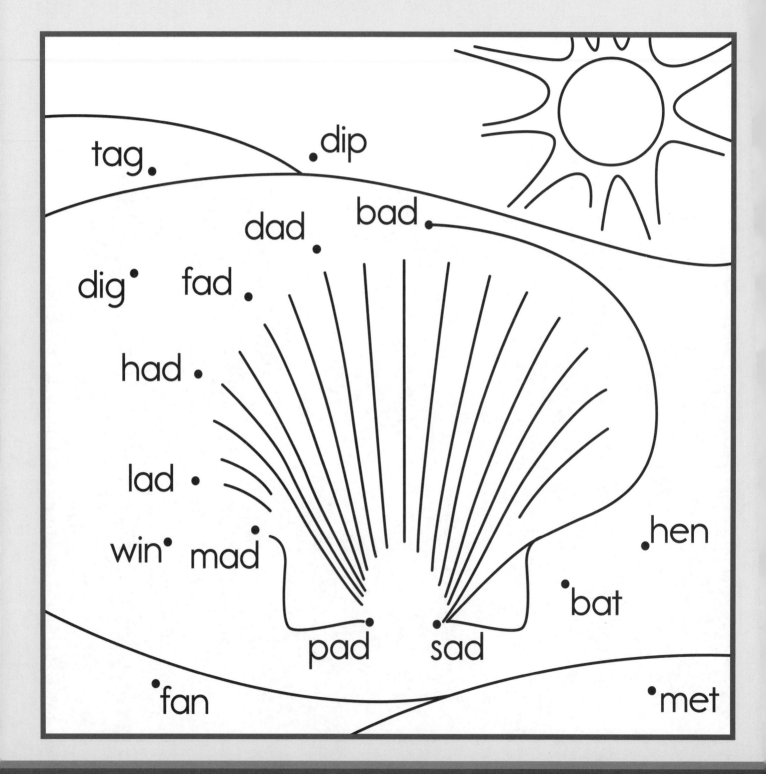

Mystery Picture

FIND the spaces with the words that sound like **ham**. COLOR those spaces blue to see the mystery picture.

HINT: You can see me in the sky at night. I am a dot of twinkling light.

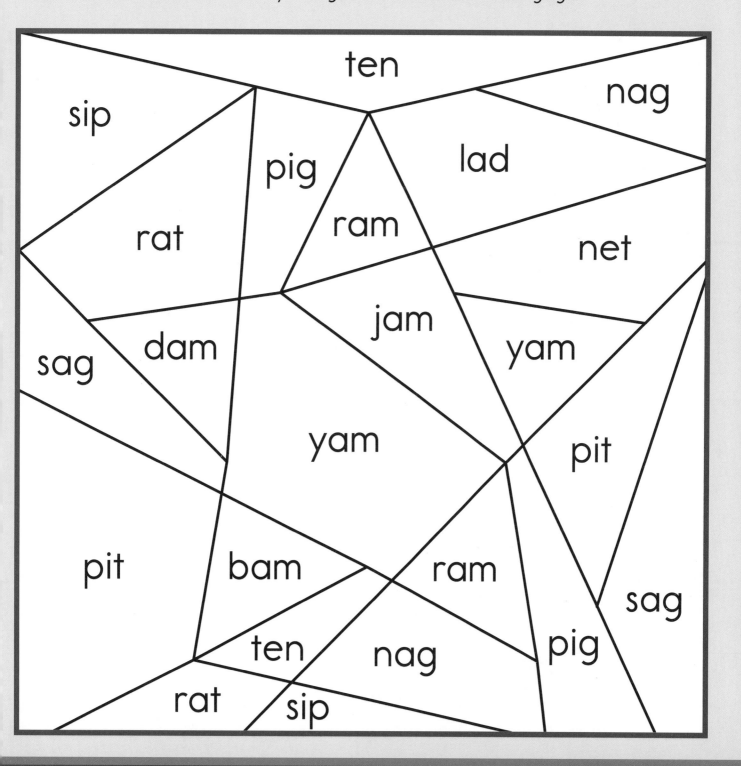

Rhyming Fun

Connect the Dots

DRAW a line to connect the words that sound like **bag**. Connect them in ABC order.

HINT: Give me to a dog to chew. He will wag his tail to say, "Thank you."

Unscramble the Rhymes

UNSCRAMBLE the letters to write a rhyme for each picture.

amr   bma

_____   _____

- - - - - - - -   - - - - - - - -

_____   _____

gba   atg

_____   _____

- - - - - - - -   - - - - - - - -

_____   _____

What Am I?

MATCH the words to the pictures.

spring

summer

fall

winter

Color by Rhyme

FOLLOW the directions to COLOR each part of the picture.

 = words that sound like **yam**

 = words that sound like **tag**

 = words that sound like **sad**

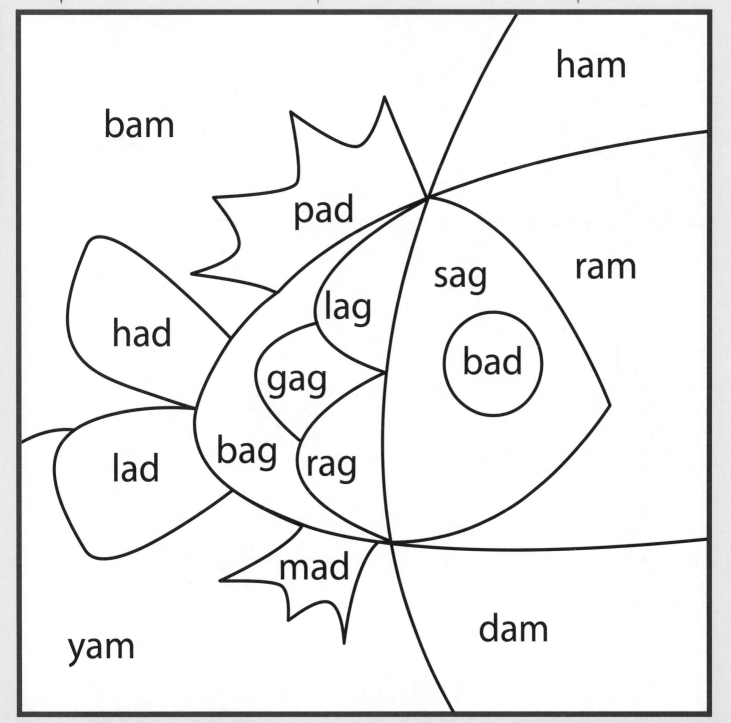

bam

ham

pad

had

lag

sag

ram

gag

bad

lad

bag

rag

mad

yam

dam

Shapes

Hide and Seek

CIRCLE the shapes hiding in the picture.

triangle   circle   diamond   square   oval   rectangle

Make a Match

CUT OUT the words and pictures. READ the rules. PLAY the game!

Rules: 2 players
1. PLACE the cards face-down on a table.
2. TAKE TURNS turning over two cards at a time.
3. KEEP the cards when you match a picture and a word.

How many matches can you collect?

square		rectangle	
oval		circle	
triangle		diamond	

Mystery Picture

FIND the spaces with the word **square**. COLOR those spaces green to see the mystery picture.

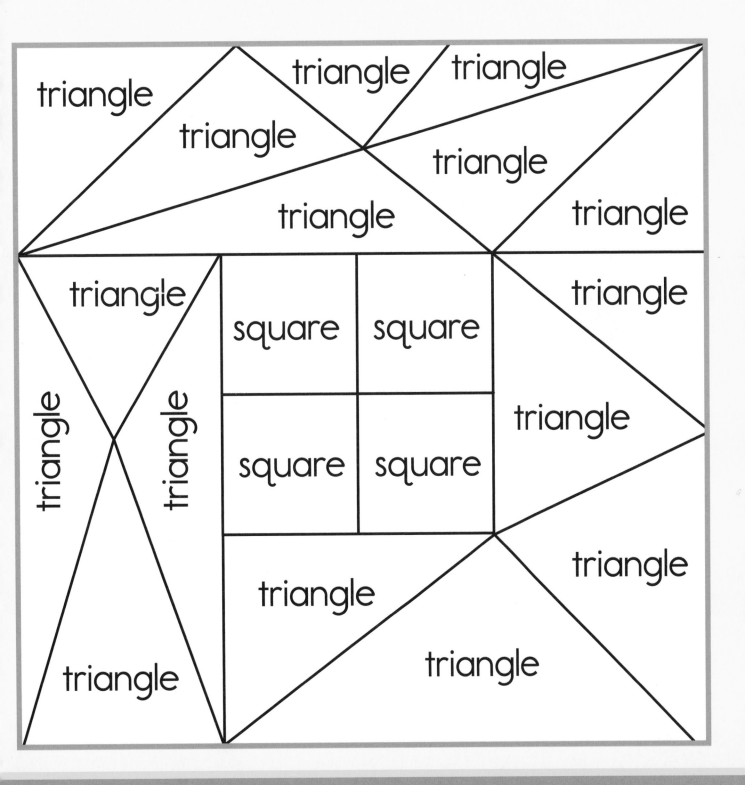

Shapes

Criss Cross

LOOK at each picture. FILL IN the missing letters to complete each shape word.

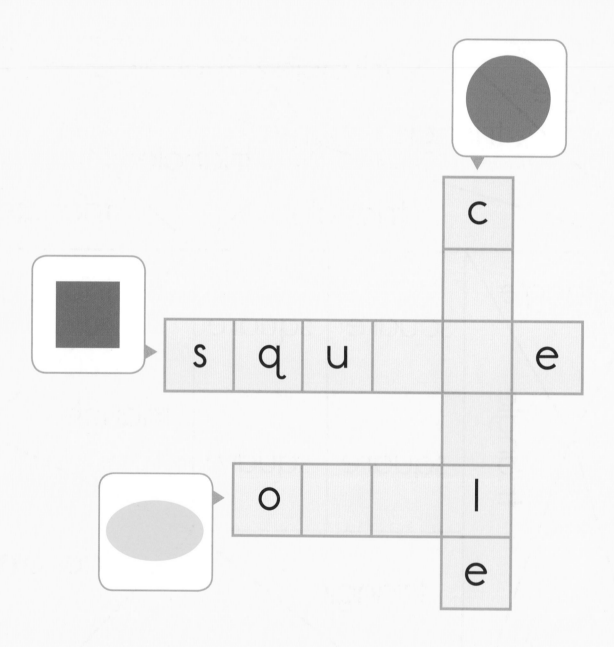

Mystery Picture

FIND the spaces with the word **diamond**. COLOR those spaces purple to see the mystery picture.

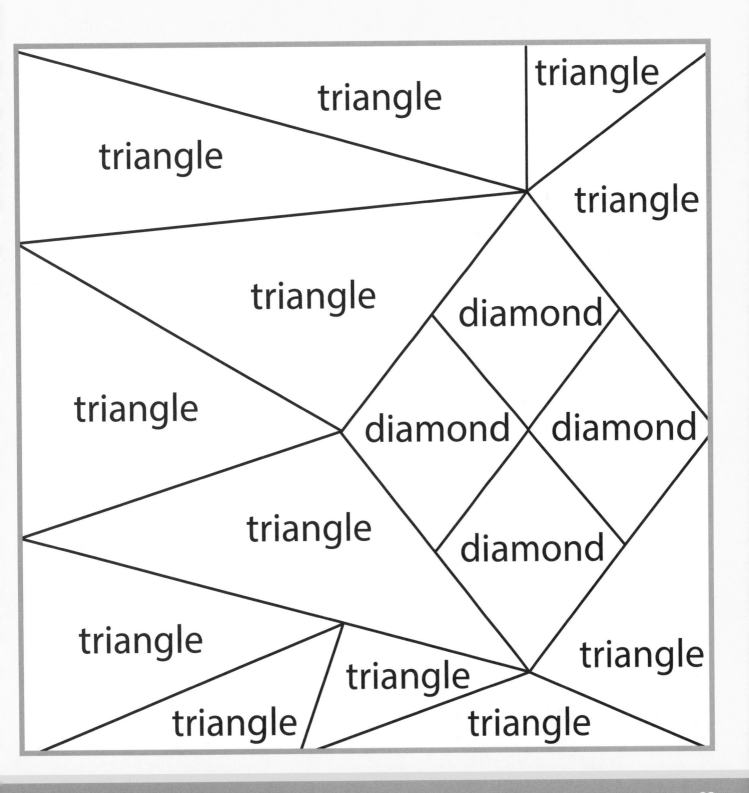

Word Hunt

CIRCLE the words in the grid that end in **-an**.
Words go across and down.

pan	can	fan	man	ran

b	e	z	m	p	r	i
k	d	g	w	t	a	o
p	a	n	c	s	n	h
u	q	f	c	j	l	n
m	v	x	a	e	b	y
a	u	g	n	k	r	l
n	p	d	o	m	i	c
f	w	q	b	f	a	n

Find the Path

DRAW a line through the words that end in **-an** to help the van get to the farm.

fresh eggs

Start

ran

pan

wag

fan

sag

sat

bag

tag

hat

can

rag

pat

mat

bat

man

End

Word Hunt

CIRCLE the words in the grid that end in **-at**.
Words go across and down.

cat	rat	fat	hat	mat	sat

i	r	a	t	z	d	q
c	p	f	w	s	u	b
e	l	r	v	a	h	m
c	a	t	y	t	o	g
s	x	e	t	n	b	z
o	f	k	d	m	a	t
r	a	i	l	f	q	j
z	t	o	h	a	t	n

Find the Path

DRAW a line through the words that end in **-at** to help the bat get to the cave.

End

cat

ham   yam   lad

fat   ram   jam

                    dam   mad

        sad

rat

                sat

        mat   Start

had

        dad

Word Endings

Word Hunt

CIRCLE the words in the grid that end in **-en**.
Words go across and down.

| den | ten | pen | men | hen |

a	r	t	p	e	n	u
h	e	n	v	s	c	m
p	l	h	i	b	o	y
n	k	j	w	d	e	n
u	m	f	q	v	z	d
r	e	q	b	k	h	t
o	n	p	g	r	l	e
k	u	y	x	s	c	n

Find the Path

DRAW a line through the words that end in **-en** to help the hen go home.

Connect the Dots

DRAW a line to connect the words that sound like **pan**. Connect them in ABC order.

HINT: Drawing pictures is what I do. I am many colors like red and blue.

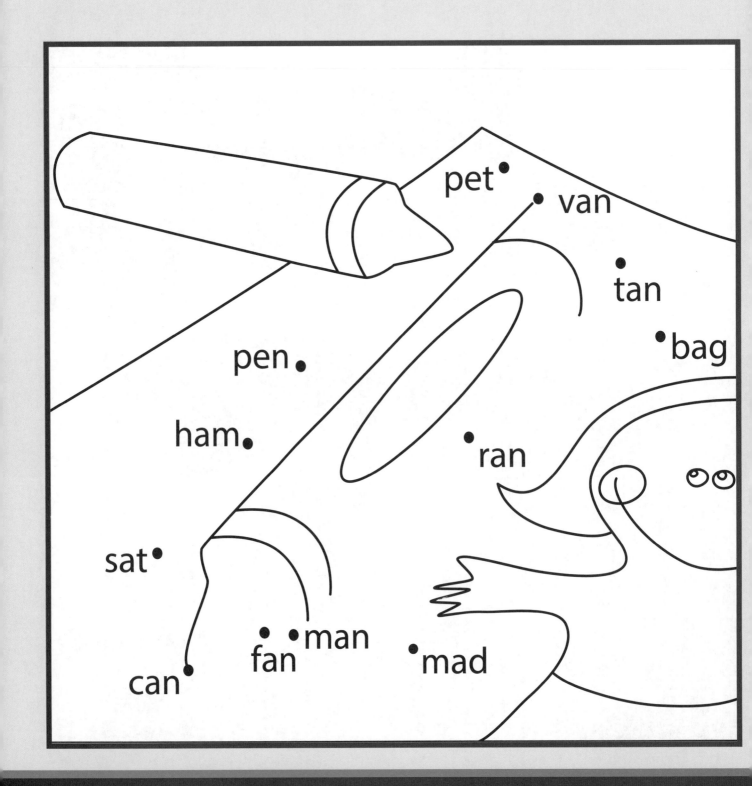

Mystery Picture

FIND the spaces with words that rhyme with **Ken**. COLOR those spaces red to see the mystery picture.

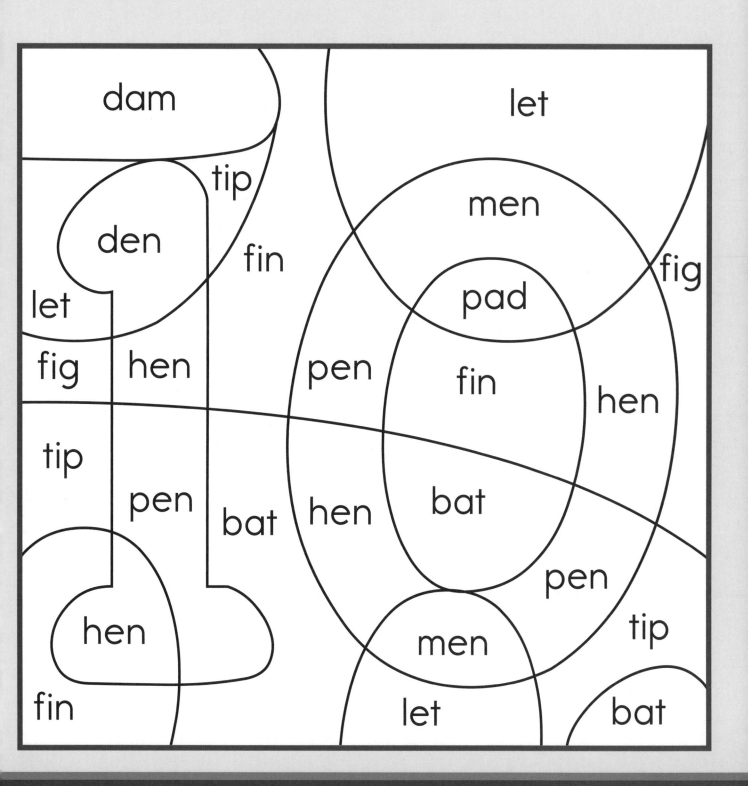

Rhyming Fun

Connect the Dots

DRAW a line to connect the words that sound like **bat**. Connect them in ABC order.

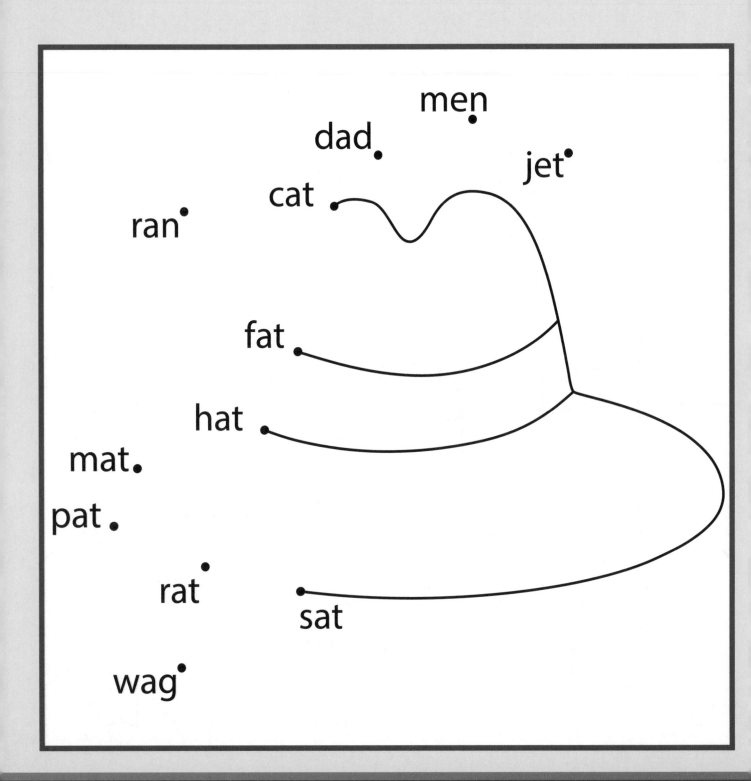

Unscramble the Rhymes

UNSCRAMBLE the letters to write a rhyme for each picture.

neh   npe

_____   _____

- - - - -   - - - - -

_____   _____

atb   hta

_____   _____

- - - - -   - - - - -

_____   _____

What Am I?

MATCH each shape word to its picture.

triangle

circle

square

oval

diamond

rectangle

Sort It Out!

CUT out the words. SORT them into groups of words that sound the same.

pan	ram	den
bag	mad	bad
cat	flag	fan
pen	sad	dam
van	wag	pad
rag	yam	tag
ham	bat	rat
hen	can	man
hat	men	lad
ten	sat	clam

Color by Rhyme

FOLLOW the directions to COLOR each part of the picture.

= words that
sound like
rat

= words that
sound like
hen

= words that
sound like
van

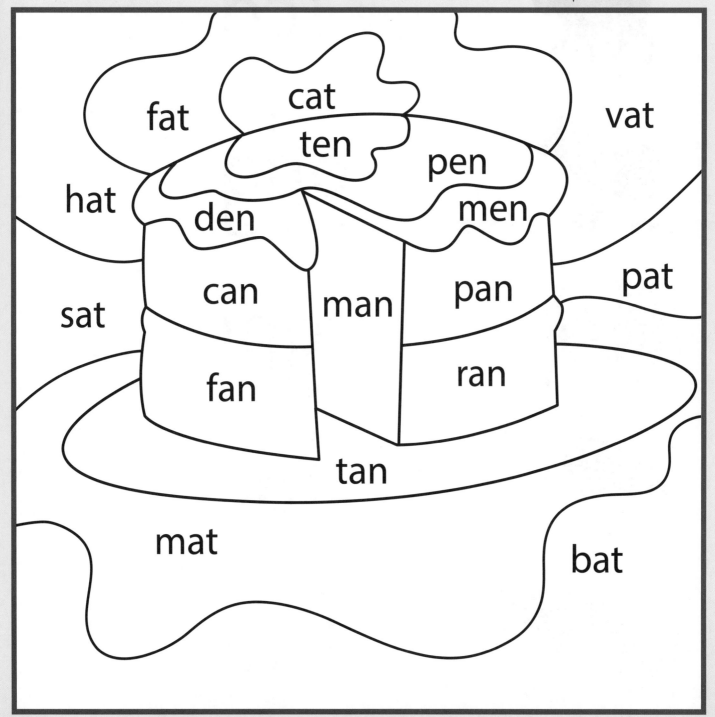

Animals

Unscramble It

UNSCRAMBLE the letters to write the word for each animal picture.

tca   cat

odg   _____

gpi   _____

tar   _____

fxo   _____

Who Am I?

MATCH each animal word to its picture.

horse

cow

bird

mouse

goat

Hide and Seek

CIRCLE the animals in the picture.

cow   horse   goat   mouse   dog   bird

Who Am I?

MATCH each animal word to its picture.

zebra

tiger

elephant

lion

monkey

Hide and Seek

CIRCLE the animals in the picture.

monkey   elephant   tiger   lion   zebra   bat

Criss Cross

LOOK at each picture. FILL IN the missing letters to complete each animal word.

Word Hunt

CIRCLE the words in the grid that end in **-et**.
Words go across and down.

pet	wet	met	jet	let	set

p	e	t	a	w	b	d
c	k	m	i	e	r	p
q	z	l	o	t	n	e
u	j	e	t	v	a	m
r	t	s	h	f	i	e
j	q	m	u	l	s	t
s	e	t	r	e	w	z
a	g	p	o	t	t	e

Find the Path

DRAW a line through the words that end in **-et** to help the fish swim to her friends.

men

big

Start

ten

get

fig

dig

set

wig

let

jet

hen

pig

den

pen

End

wet

Word Hunt

CIRCLE the words in the grid that end in **-ig**.
Words go across and down.

-ig

wig	pig	fig	big	dig	jig

p	d	f	j	i	g	r
i	q	e	m	n	s	a
g	p	h	r	b	i	u
v	x	w	a	i	o	w
f	i	g	e	g	t	i
s	r	n	c	p	e	g
u	b	d	i	g	k	x
y	f	e	n	f	q	r

Find the Path

DRAW a line through the words that end in **-ig** to help the pig into the pen.

End

dig

jet

wet

fig

pet

tin

net

wig

set

pin

bin

jig

win

Start

big

fin

Word Hunt

CIRCLE the words in the grid that end in **-in**.
Words go across and down.

| pin | fin | win | kin | tin | bin |

a	d	z	x	b	f	c
t	y	u	p	e	i	h
i	f	v	i	t	n	s
n	g	j	n	k	r	p
q	l	m	o	e	t	w
w	i	n	y	k	f	h
a	r	v	u	i	b	k
b	i	n	s	n	q	d

Find the Path

DRAW a line through the words that end in **-in** to help the tiger through the grass.

Start

rip

fig

hip

tin

bin

fin

wig

sip

win

dig

tip

kin

pig

End

lip

Rhyming Fun

Connect the Dots

DRAW a line to connect the words that sound like **pin**. Connect them in ABC order.

HINT: I am round and lots of fun. Sometimes, I make you run.

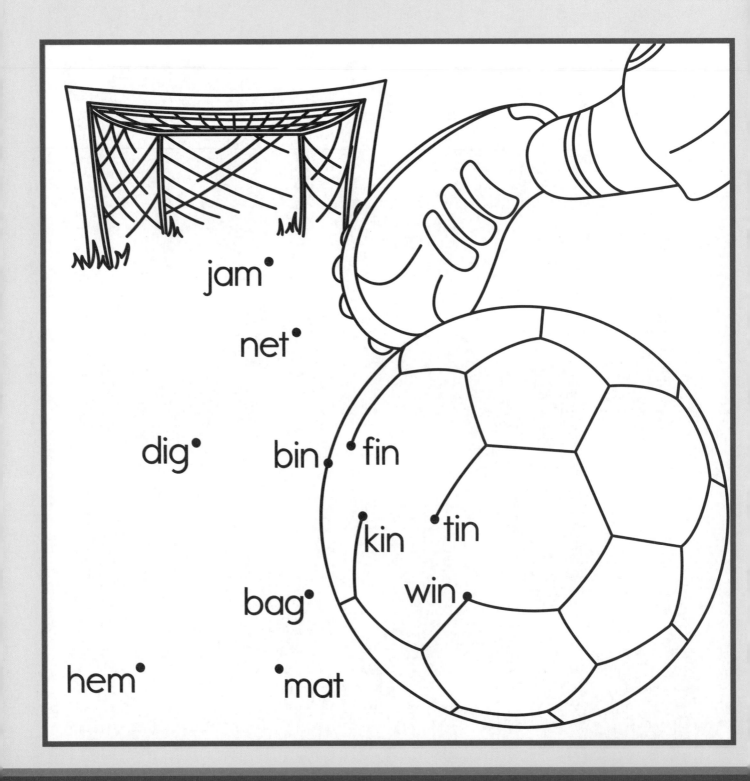

jam

net

dig   bin   fin

              kin   tin

        bag   win

hem   mat

Mystery Picture

FIND the spaces with words that sound like **pet**. COLOR those spaces red to see the mystery picture.

HINT: I am a fruit from a tree. I crunch when you bite into me.

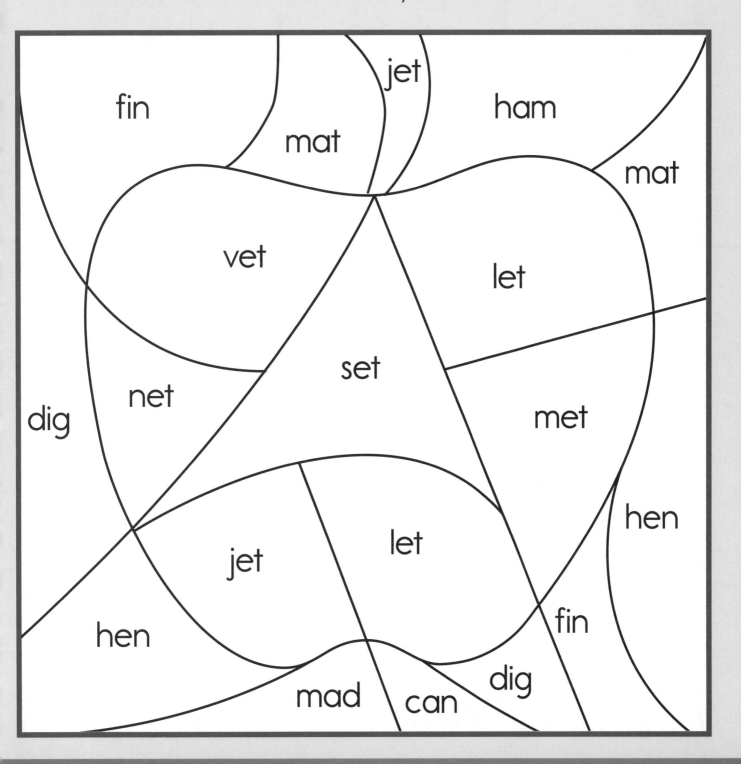

Rhyming Fun

Connect the Dots

DRAW a line to connect the words that sound like **pig**. Connect them in ABC order.

HINT: I am a shape that says, "I love you." Red is my favorite color too.

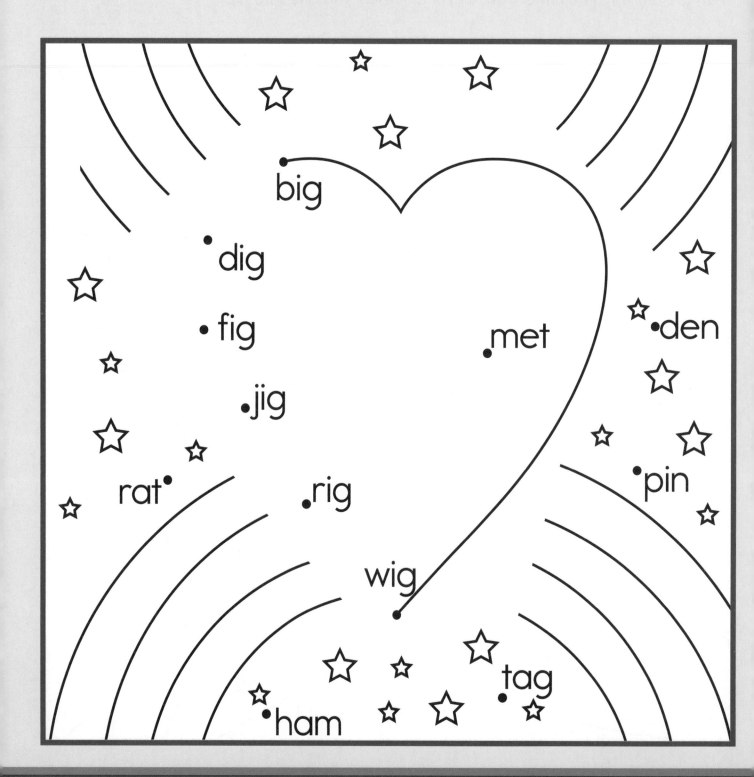

Unscramble the Rhymes

UNSCRAMBLE the letters to write a rhyme for each picture.

twe   ept

_____   _____

- - - - - - - - - - -   - - - - - - - - - - -

_____   _____

igb   giw

_____   _____

- - - - - - - - - - -   - - - - - - - - - - -

_____   _____

Word Hunt

CIRCLE the animal words in the grid. Words go across and down.

| cow | horse | goat | lion | fox | monkey |

b	c	h	o	r	s	e
g	o	r	e	q	z	w
v	w	i	l	n	o	f
y	p	m	u	d	t	o
g	o	a	t	y	r	x
n	a	p	l	i	o	n
q	u	k	g	c	f	l
m	o	n	k	e	y	i

Color by Rhyme

FOLLOW the directions to COLOR each part of the picture.

 = words that sound like **pin**

 = words that sound like **pig**

 = words that sound like **pet**

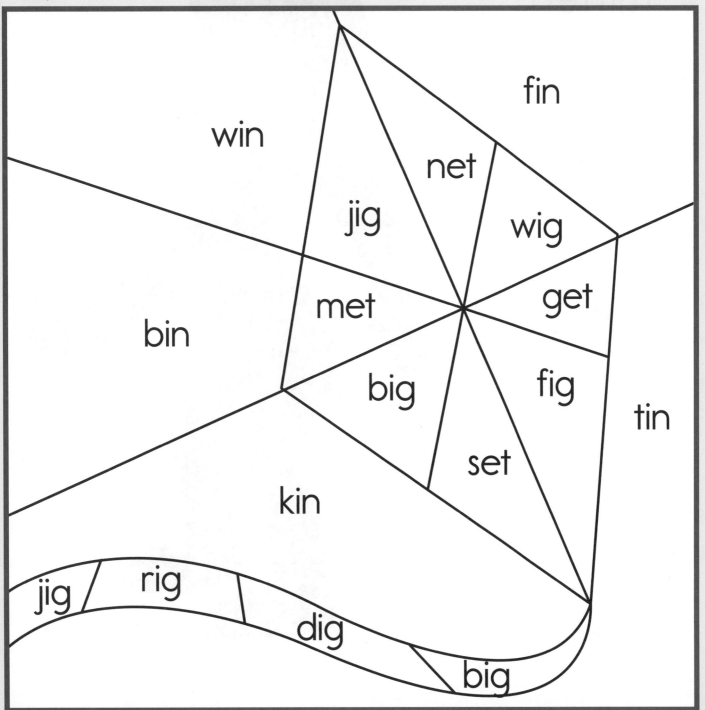

What to Wear?

Label the Clothing

DRAW a line from each word to an item of clothing on the boy.

mitten

pants

hat

boot

sweater

Label the Clothing

DRAW a line from each word to an item of clothing on the girl.

skirt

shirt

socks

shoes

belt

What to Wear?

Unscramble It

UNSCRAMBLE the letters to write the word for each clothing picture.

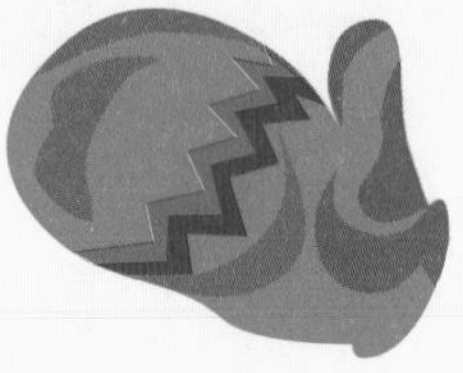

ittmen

_____

1

aht

_____

2

tspan

_____

3

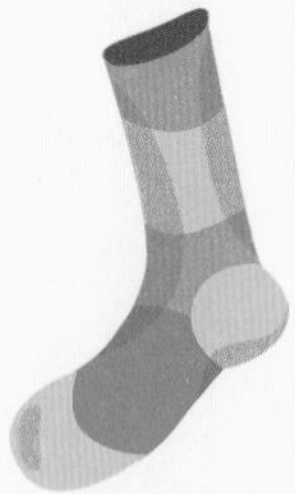

ckso

_____

4

ssdre

_____

5

Hide and Seek

FIND and CIRCLE each item of clothing in the picture.

shoes	shirt	belt	sock	pants	hat

What to Wear?

Word Hunt

CIRCLE each clothing word in the grid. Words go across and down.

hat	dress	mitten	boot	shirt	sweater

```
p  b  o  o  t  e  s
h  a  t  q  b  c  w
d  r  i  d  k  n  e
s  j  g  r  w  f  a
h  l  a  e  h  o  t
i  u  x  s  y  d  e
r  z  r  s  c  m  r
t  m  i  t  t  e  n
```

Criss Cross

LOOK at each picture. FILL IN the missing letters to complete the clothing words.

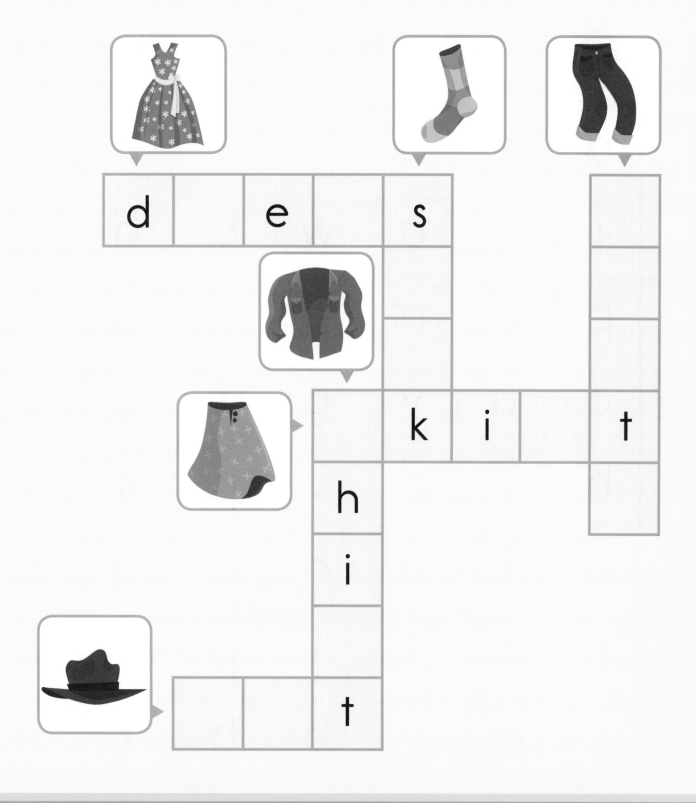

Word Endings

Word Hunt

CIRCLE the words in the grid that end in **-ip**.
Words go across and down.

dip	hip	lip	rip	tip	zip

d	o	q	r	i	p	k
i	m	a	w	b	d	r
p	o	n	p	l	u	h
c	u	y	g	i	e	z
h	i	p	v	p	s	i
w	k	u	q	c	g	p
a	p	t	i	p	j	t
r	m	y	b	h	x	e

Find the Path

FOLLOW the path marked with words ending in **-ip** to help the goat cross the bridge.

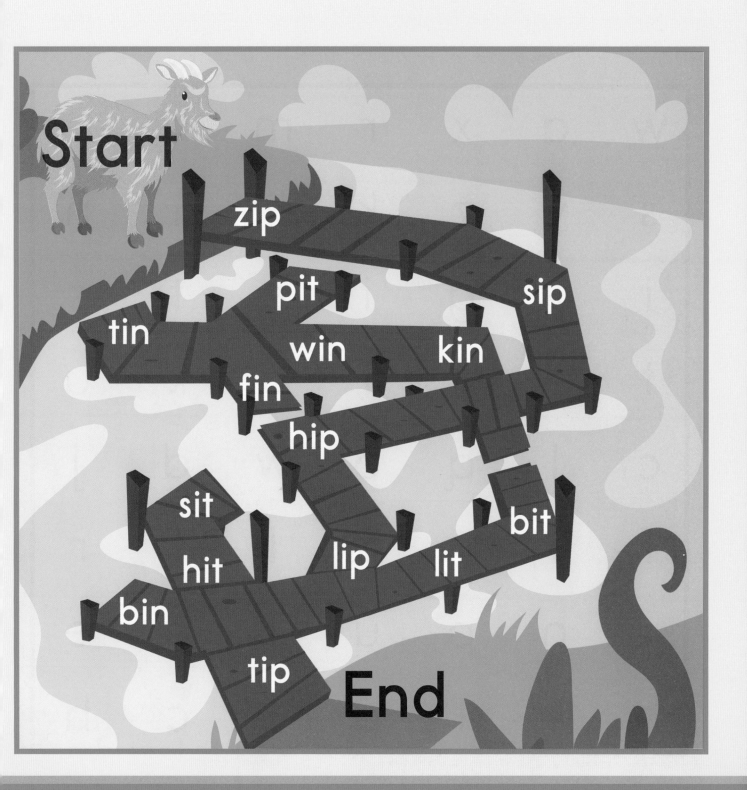

Word Hunt

CIRCLE the words in the grid that end in -it.
Words go across and down.

bit	kit	sit	fit	lit	hit

w	a	x	r	m	b	e
s	v	z	k	h	i	n
i	y	g	i	e	t	s
t	t	f	t	b	k	u
c	l	q	o	w	d	j
f	i	t	m	l	f	r
v	n	p	u	i	b	e
h	i	t	a	t	c	h

Find the Path

FOLLOW the path marked with words ending in **-it** to help the mouse get the cheese.

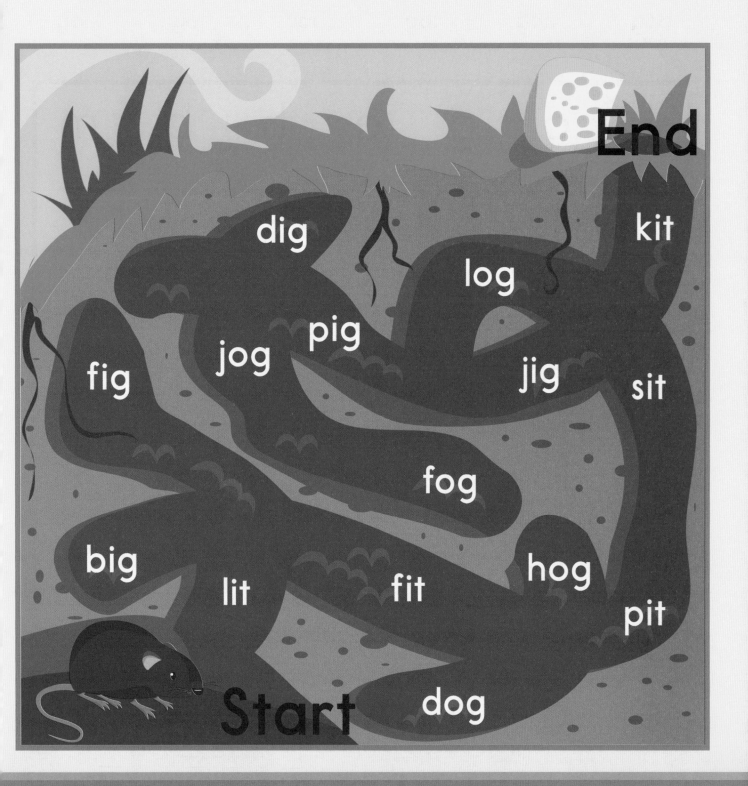

Word Hunt

-og

CIRCLE the words in the grid that end in **-og**.
Words go across and down.

bog	dog	fog	hog	jog	log

l	o	g	e	h	b	m
x	f	l	y	o	a	c
d	n	k	z	g	r	v
t	b	o	g	s	i	d
q	p	a	j	w	u	o
b	l	v	r	f	t	g
j	o	g	s	o	c	h
e	d	p	y	g	x	i

Find the Path

FOLLOW the path marked with words ending in **-og** to help the dog to the log.

Connect the Dots

DRAW a line to connect the words that sound like **pit**. Connect them in ABC order.

HINT: I am seen in the sky at night. I change size and my color is white.

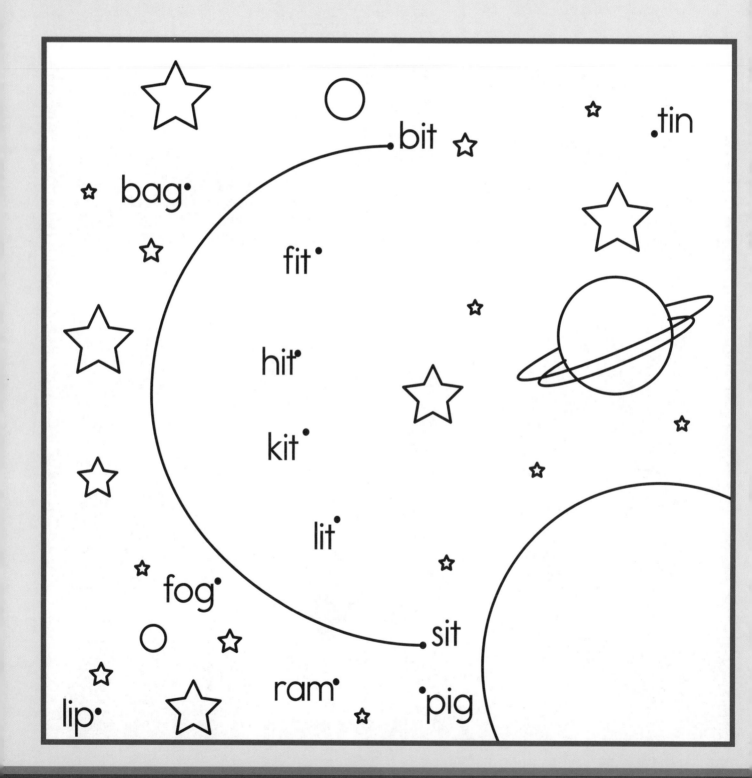

Mystery Picture

FIND the spaces with words that sound like **dip**. COLOR those spaces yellow to see the mystery picture.

HINT: I give the day its light. I am hot and very bright.

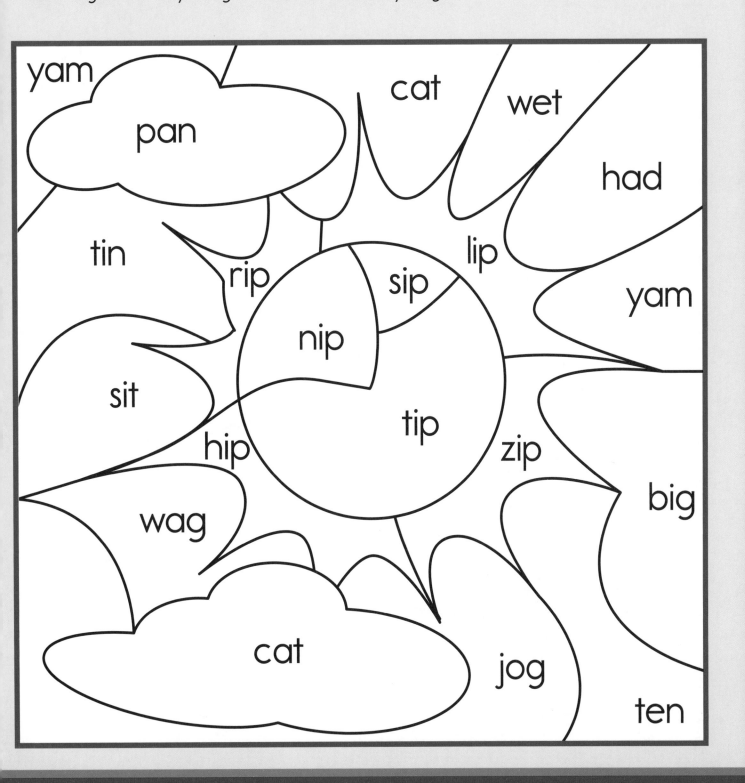

Connect the Dots

DRAW a line to connect the words that sound like **fog**. Connect them in ABC order.

HINT: I used to be part of a tree. There's a hole inside of me.

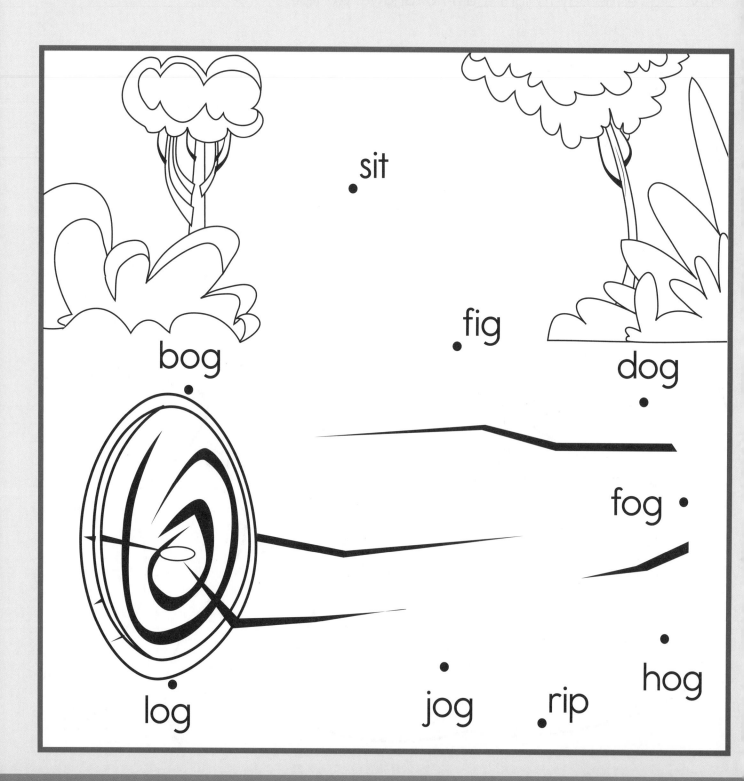

sit

fig

bog

dog

log

fog

jog   rip   hog

Unscramble the Rhymes

UNSCRAMBLE the letters to write a rhyme for each picture.

odg   goj

_____   _____

- - - - - - - - - - - -   - - - - - - - - - - - -

_____   _____

gip   ijg

_____   _____

- - - - - - - - - - - -   - - - - - - - - - - - -

_____   _____

Review

Hide and Seek

LOOK at the words. FIND and CIRCLE each one in the picture.

monkey shirt pants horse dress shoe zebra bird

Sort It Out

CUT OUT the words. SORT them into groups of words that sound the same.

bet	dip	wet
bin	log	jog
fog	win	tin
tip	hit	sip
fit	pet	hog
jet	dog	pit
lip	hip	rip
set	kit	net
sit	pin	lit
fin	get	bog

Color by Rhyme

FOLLOW the directions to COLOR each part of the picture.

 = words
that sound
like **dip**

 = words
that sound
like **net**

 = words
that sound
like **pig**

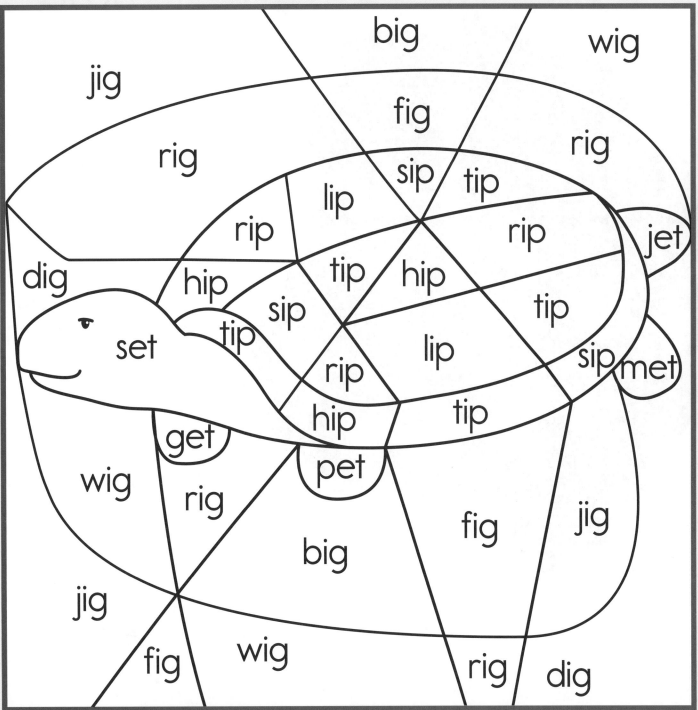

The Body

Label the Parts

MATCH the words to the picture. DRAW a line from each word to the right part of the girl's face.

nose

eye

mouth

hair

ear

Label the Parts

MATCH the words to the picture. DRAW a line from each word to the right part of the boy's body.

head

neck

arm

leg

hand

foot

The Body

Match Up

MATCH each word to the right picture.

hand

eye

nose

foot

ear

Make a Match

CUT OUT the words and pictures. READ the rules. PLAY the game!

Rules: 2 players
1. PLACE the cards face-down on a table.
2. TAKE TURNS turning over two cards at a time.
3. KEEP the cards when you match a picture and a word.

How many matches can you collect?

arm		ear	
hand		mouth	
eye		nose	
foot		leg	

The Body

Criss Cross

LOOK at each picture. FILL IN the missing letters to complete each word.

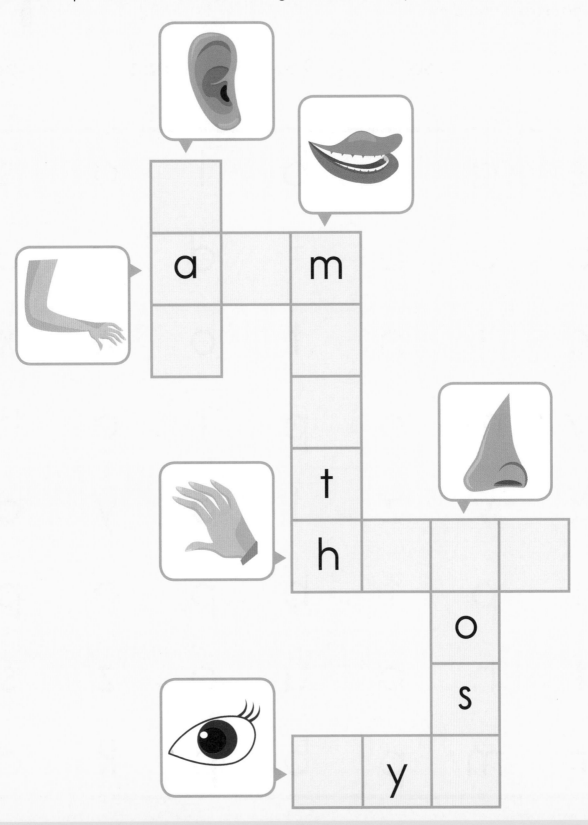

Word Hunt

CIRCLE the words in the grid that end in **-op**.
Words go across and down.

-op

| bop | hop | top | mop | pop |

e	q	r	b	l	a	s
b	o	p	f	d	m	u
c	j	n	t	o	w	x
y	m	o	p	i	g	h
k	v	z	l	a	y	o
i	p	t	b	p	e	p
f	h	o	u	o	z	s
r	m	p	b	p	k	d

Find the Path

DRAW a line through the words that end in **-op** to help the kangaroo hop to the top of the hill.

Word Hunt

CIRCLE the words in the grid that end in -ot.
Words go across and down.

lot	pot	rot	hot	not	dot

a	z	q	c	l	r	k
e	n	b	l	f	o	m
s	o	d	o	u	t	x
f	t	m	t	v	w	p
h	j	u	a	p	i	o
r	c	h	o	t	s	t
y	q	g	f	o	h	l
d	o	t	t	v	f	a

Find the Path

DRAW a line through the words that end in **-ot** to help the butterfly get to the flowers.

Start

cot

low   mow

dot

mop

bow

pop   got

top

hot

bop

not

hop   row   tow

End

Word Hunt

CIRCLE the words in the grid that end in **-ow**.
Words go across and down.

bow	low	mow	row	tow

a	e	z	x	d	b	h
r	y	u	t	e	o	c
o	f	r	o	n	w	p
w	g	v	w	j	k	w
i	l	m	h	e	t	s
m	o	w	y	l	f	h
a	r	v	u	o	b	k
t	n	i	s	w	q	d

Find the Path

DRAW a line through the words that end in **-ow** to help the girl row the boat to shore.

Start

rot

tow   cub   bow   pot

low   row   hot

hub

sub

got

tub   rub   mow

not

End

Connect the Dots

DRAW a line to connect the words that sound like **pop**. Connect them in ABC order.

HINT: I like to climb to the **top** of these.

Mystery Picture

FIND the spaces with words that sound like **hot**. COLOR those spaces orange to see the mystery picture.

HINT: I am orange and fun to munch. I am a good part of lunch.

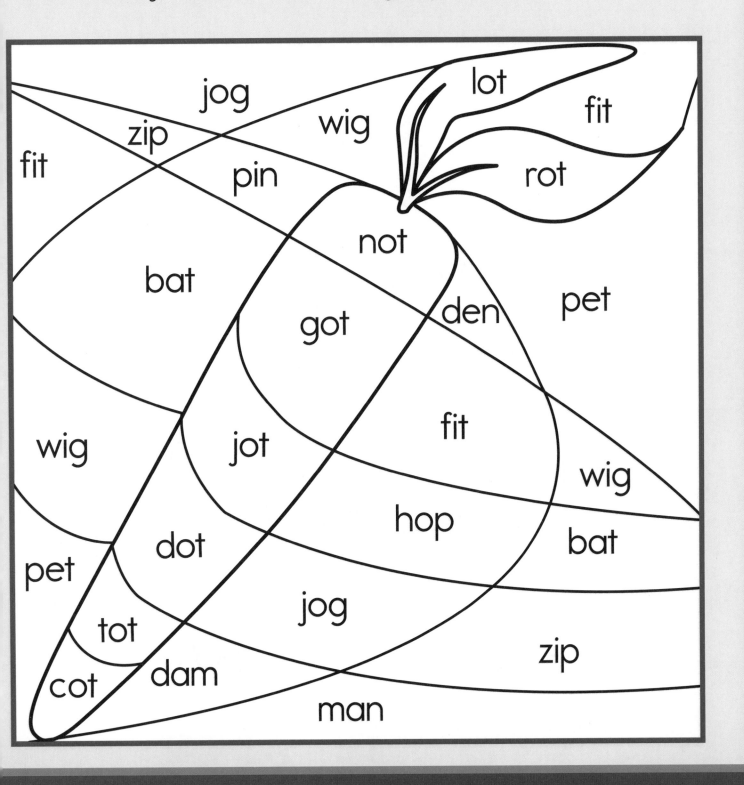

Connect the Dots

DRAW a line to connect the words that sound like **row**. Connect them in ABC order.

HINT: The wind will help you go, so you don't have to **row**.

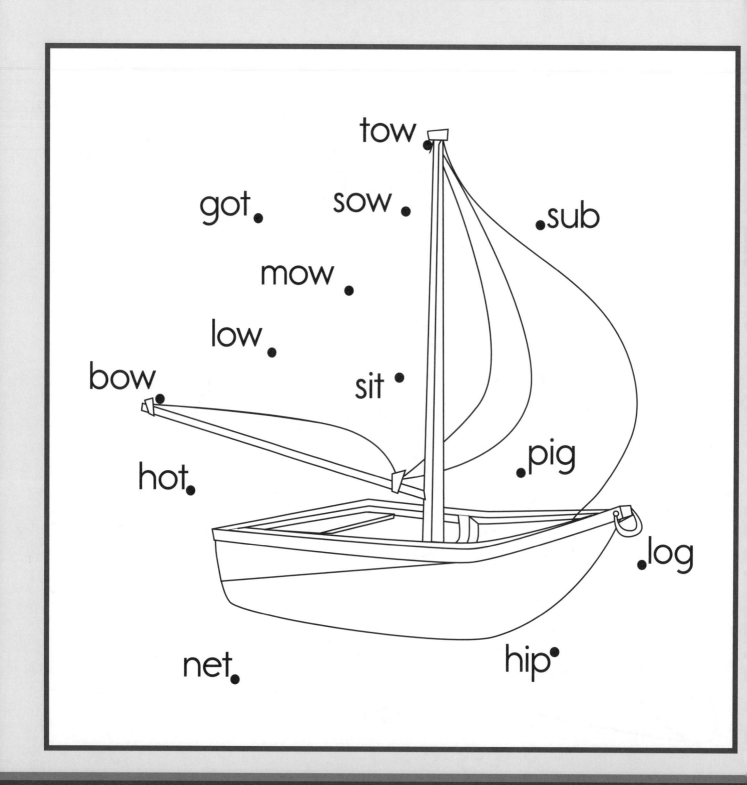

Unscramble the Rhymes

UNSCRAMBLE the letters to write a rhyme for each picture.

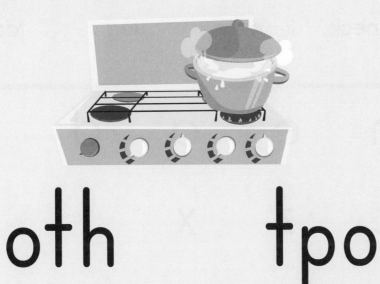

oth   tpo

_____   _____

- - - - - - - - - -   - - - - - - - - - -

_____   _____

wbo   wor

_____   _____

- - - - - - - - - -   - - - - - - - - - -

_____   _____

Word Hunt

CIRCLE each body part word in the grid. Words go across and down.

head	neck	nose	leg	foot	ear

g	h	e	a	d	l	n
b	c	z	x	i	p	o
n	e	c	k	q	r	s
a	v	m	b	u	w	e
l	n	f	o	o	t	k
e	f	e	s	j	p	z
g	q	t	d	i	v	b
a	k	o	e	a	r	n

Color by Rhyme

COLOR each part of the picture.

 = words that sound like **row**

 = words that sound like **mop**

= words that sound like **dot**

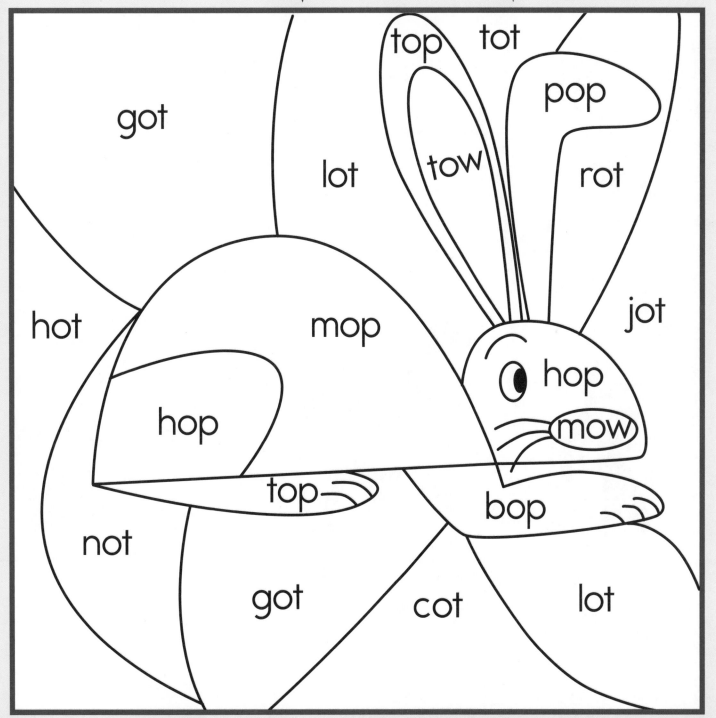

Food

Hide and Seek

LOOK at the words. FIND and CIRCLE each one in the picture.

egg   carrot   apple   pizza   banana   bread   cake

Unscramble It

UNSCRAMBLE the letters to write the word for each picture.

gge

_____

1

pplea

_____

2

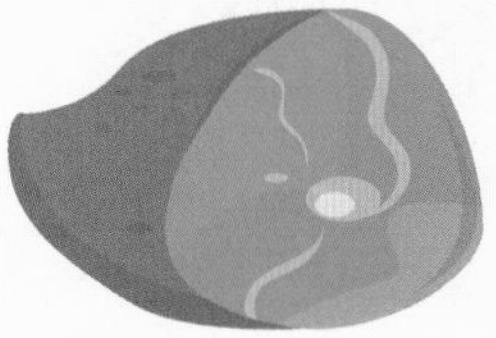

ahm

_____

3

anaban

_____

4

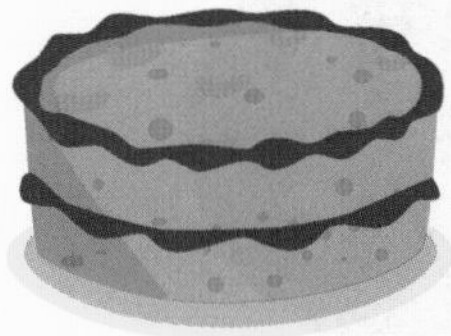

keca

_____

5

Food

What Am I?

MATCH each word to its picture.

bread

lemon

tomato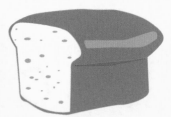

carrot

pizza

Make a Match

CUT OUT the words and pictures. READ the rules. PLAY the game!

Rules: 2 players
1. PLACE the cards face-down on a table.
2. TAKE TURNS turning over two cards at a time.
3. KEEP the cards when you match a picture and a word.

How many matches can you collect?

apple		egg	
banana		cake	
carrot		orange	
bread		lemon	

Food

Criss Cross

LOOK at each picture. FILL IN the missing letters to complete each food word.

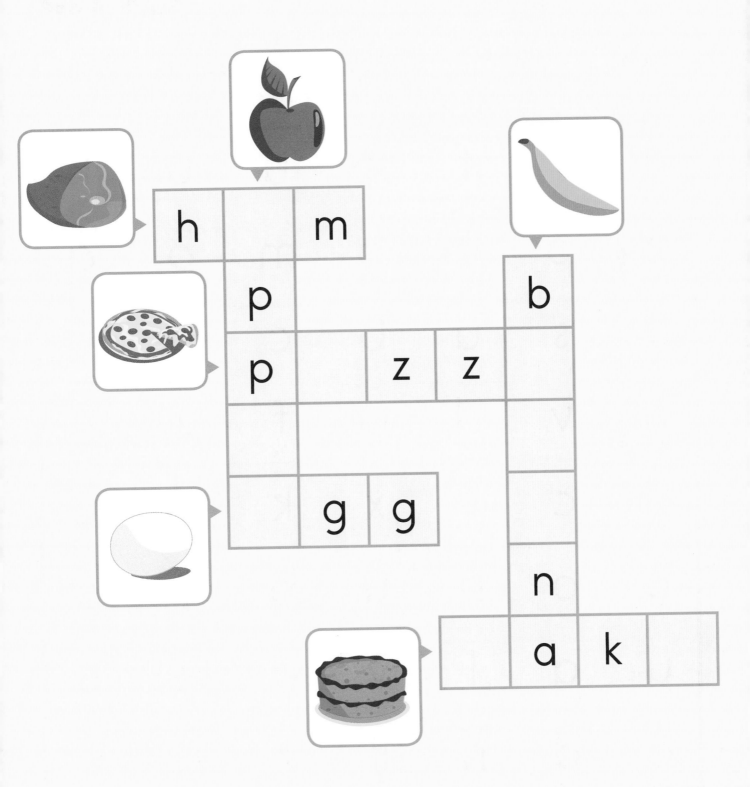

Word Hunt

CIRCLE the words in the grid that end in **-ub**.
Words go across and down.

cub	hub	rub	sub	tub

a	l	t	t	u	b	k
s	p	e	b	m	o	q
j	s	u	b	c	h	i
g	v	d	w	f	z	r
u	c	r	x	k	i	u
c	o	h	u	b	y	b
u	a	l	v	d	x	e
b	d	n	r	z	u	f

Find the Path

DRAW a line through the words that end in **-ub** to help the cub find his mom.

Start

rub

bug

tug

sub

row

bow

tub

hug

tow

cub

mow

low

mug

End

hub

rug

Word Hunt

CIRCLE the words in the grid that end in **-ug**.
Words go across and down.

-ug

| bug | dug | hug | mug | rug | tug |

c	f	m	o	x	d	p
b	e	n	h	i	u	w
u	h	i	u	t	g	q
g	a	l	g	d	w	b
k	n	v	i	r	u	z
r	u	g	a	m	f	l
e	d	s	x	u	q	g
t	u	g	z	g	e	h

Find the Path

DRAW a line through the words that end in **-ug** to help the bug cross the rug.

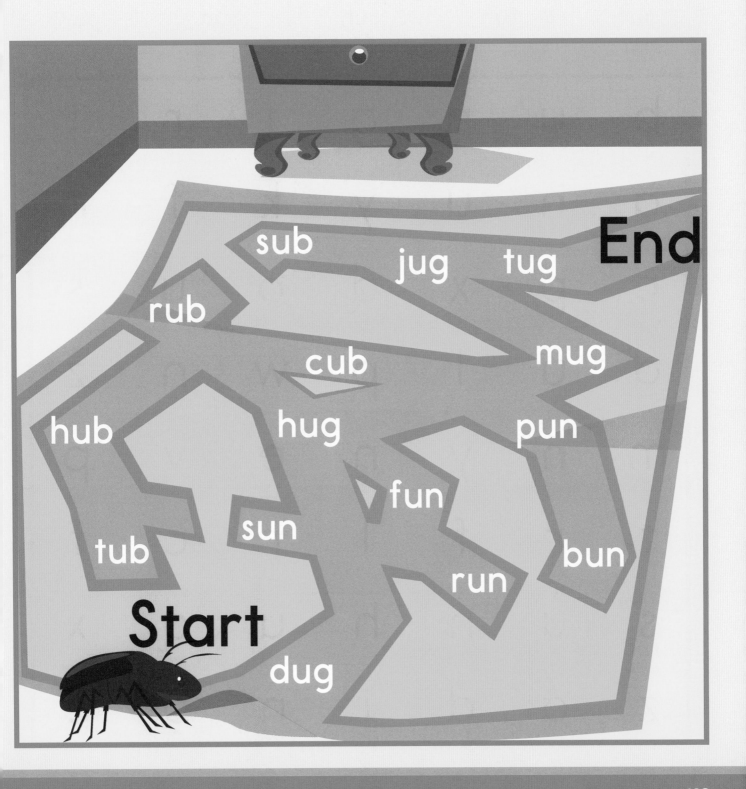

Word Hunt

CIRCLE the words in the grid that end in **-un**.
Words go across and down.

bun	fun	run	sun	pun

b	u	n	g	i	r	t
a	h	u	y	k	f	n
c	p	x	q	o	u	s
d	u	l	p	w	n	z
m	n	y	n	e	v	p
t	r	f	l	r	c	f
s	u	n	h	u	q	x
z	a	d	i	n	b	e

Find the Path

DRAW a line through the words that end in **-un** to help the boy run the race.

Start

bug

hug

sun

hut

tug

bun

nut

but

cut

rug

rut

fun

mug

run

pun

FINISH LINE

End

Word Hunt

CIRCLE the words in the grid that end in **-ut**.
Words go across and down.

cut	gut	hut	nut	rut

a	z	q	y	c	i	t
s	l	p	v	u	k	w
r	u	t	o	t	r	n
b	f	m	h	e	x	g
t	g	d	k	v	i	u
o	l	n	s	h	z	t
n	u	t	q	u	e	r
y	w	a	m	t	b	u

Find the Path

DRAW a line through the words that end in **-ut** to help the squirrel get the nut.

Rhyming Fun

Unscramble the Rhymes

UNSCRAMBLE the letters to write a rhyme for each picture.

buc

_____

- - - - - - - - - - -

_____

usb

_____

- - - - - - - - - - -

_____

bgu

_____

- - - - - - - - - - -

_____

utg

_____

- - - - - - - - - - -

_____

Connect the Dots

DRAW a line to connect the words that sound like **rug**. Connect them in ABC order.

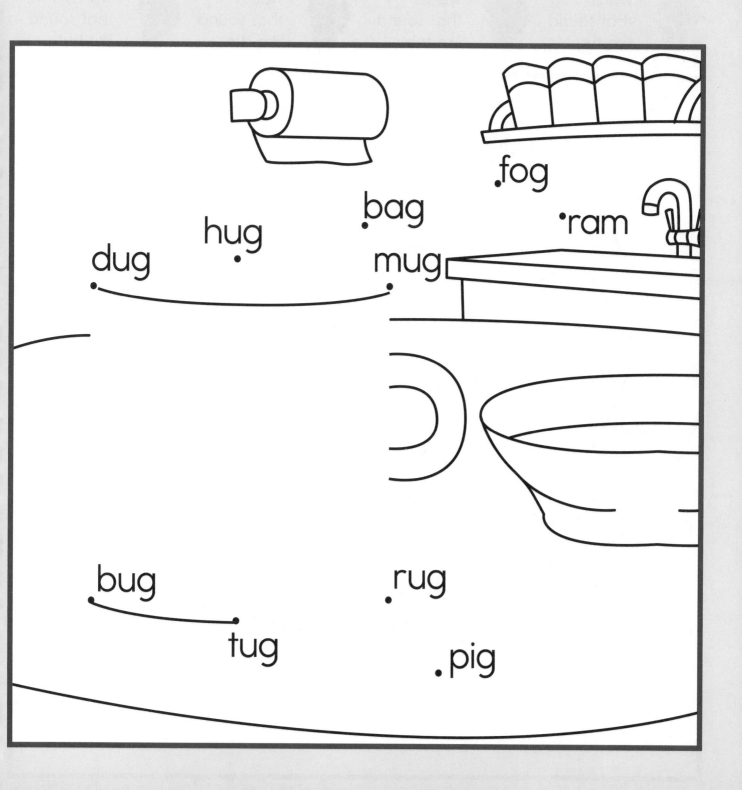

fog

bag

hug   ram

dug   mug

bug

tug   rug

pig

Rhyming Fun

Color by Rhyme

COLOR each part of the picture.

 = words that sound like **tug**

 = words that sound like **tub**

 = words that sound like **run**

 = words that sound like **hut**

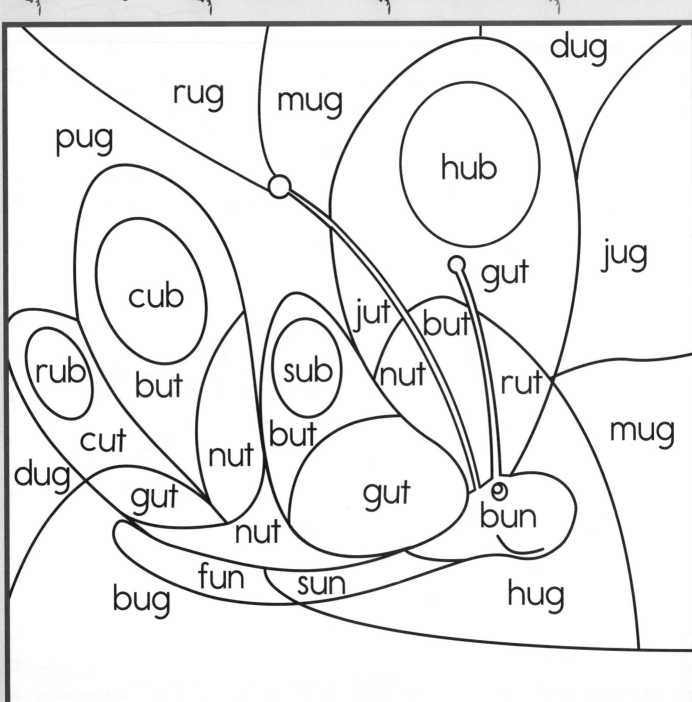

Unscramble the Rhymes

UNSCRAMBLE the letters to write a rhyme for each picture.

usn   nuf

_____

- - - - - - - - - - - - -

_____

ctu   ntu

_____

- - - - - - - - - - - - -

_____

Pick the Place

MATCH each picture to the word that best describes it.

over

under

front

back

Hide and Seek

LOOK at the words. FIND and CIRCLE each one in the picture.

pot   net   rat   mop   bug   cup

Hide and Seek

LOOK at the words. FIND and CIRCLE each one in the picture.

| pig | tub | log | cat | fan | bow |

Word Hunt

CIRCLE each place word in the grid. Words go across and down.

over   under   front   back

b	a	c	k	a	f	s
e	q	r	b	m	r	u
z	u	l	t	w	o	x
y	n	o	p	g	n	h
k	d	z	l	y	t	i
i	e	t	b	p	e	p
s	r	e	o	v	e	r
r	m	p	c	l	k	d

Criss Cross

LOOK at each picture. FILL IN the missing letters to complete the words.

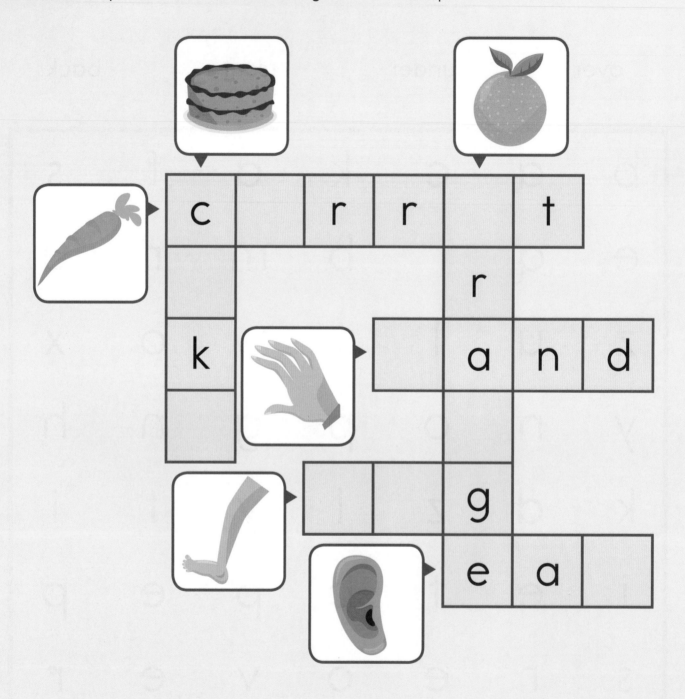

Unscramble It

UNSCRAMBLE the letters to write the word for each picture.

uns

_____
1

gur

_____
2

obw

_____
3

pto

_____
4

otp

_____
5

Answers

Page 2

Page 7

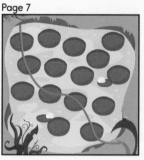

Page 12

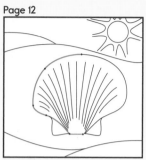

Page 18

Page 3

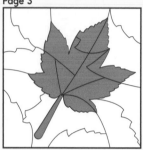

Page 8

a	e	z	x	d	s	h
w	y	u	r	e	a	c
a	c	r	a	s	g	p
g	b	v	g	j	k	w
i	l	m	h	e	t	s
b	a	g	y	t	f	h
o	r	v	u	a	b	k
t	n	i	s	g	q	d

Page 13

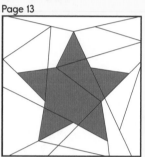

Page 21

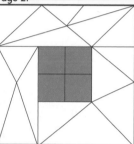

Page 4

Page 9

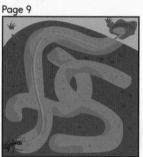

Page 14

Page 22

			c	
			i	
s	q	u	a	r	e
			c	
	o	v	a	l	e
			e	

Page 5

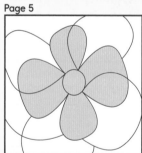

Page 10

h	a	m	e	y	b	d
c	k	m	i	a	r	p
q	z	x	o	m	n	e
u	d	a	m	v	o	j
r	t	s	h	f	i	a
j	q	c	u	l	s	m
r	a	m	r	e	w	z
a	g	p	o	t	t	e

Page 15

ram bam, bag tag

Page 16

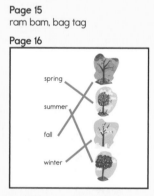

spring
summer
fall
winter

Page 23

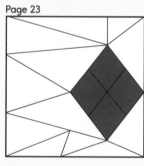

Page 6

a	z	q	c	l	h	k
e	b	n	s	a	a	m
s	a	f	a	f	d	x
f	d	m	d	u	w	d
h	j	u	o	p	i	a
r	c	m	a	d	s	d
y	q	g	f	o	e	l
p	a	d	t	v	b	a

Page 11

Page 17

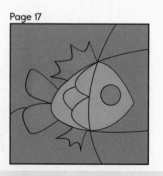

Page 24

b	e	z	m	p	r	i
k	d	g	w	t	a	o
p	a	n	c	s	n	h
u	q	f	c	n	l	n
m	v	x	a	e	b	y
a	u	g	n	k	r	l
n	p	d	o	m	i	c
f	w	q	b	f	a	n

118

Answers

Page 25

Page 26

i	r	a	t	z	d	q
c	p	f	w	s	u	b
e	l	r	v	a	h	o
c	a	t	y	t	o	g
s	x	e	t	n	b	z
o	f	k	d	m	a	t
r	a	i	l	f	q	j
z	t	o	h	a	t	n

Page 27

Page 28

a	r	t	p	e	n	u
h	e	n	v	s	c	m
p	l	h	i	b	o	y
n	k	j	w	d	e	n
u	m	f	q	v	z	d
r	e	q	b	k	h	t
o	n	p	g	r	l	e
k	u	y	x	s	c	n

Page 29

Page 30

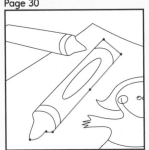

Page 31

Page 32

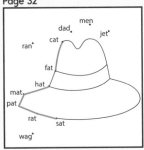

dad, men, ran, cat, jet, fat, hat, mat, pat, rat, sat, wag

Page 33

hen pen, bat hat

Page 34

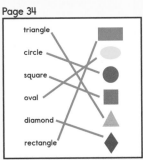

triangle, circle, square, oval, diamond, rectangle

Page 35

-an: pan, van, can, fan, man
-ag: bag, rag, flag, wag, tag
-at: cat, hat, bat, sat, rat
-en: pen, hen, ten, men, den
-am: ham, ram, yam, dam, clam
-ad: mad, sad, bad, pad, lad

Page 37

Page 38

cat, dog, pig, rat, fox

Page 39

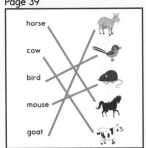

horse, cow, bird, mouse, goat

Page 40

Page 41

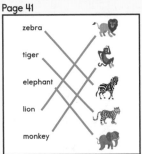

zebra, tiger, elephant, lion, monkey

Page 42

Page 43

z
e
zebra — bird
r — d
cat
l — tiger
i
mouse
n — e
r

Page 44

p	e	t	a	w	b	d
c	k	m	i	e	r	p
q	z	l	o	t	n	e
u	j	e	t	v	a	m
r	t	s	h	f	i	e
j	q	m	u	l	t	t
s	e	t	r	e	w	z
a	g	p	o	t	t	e

Page 45

Page 46

p	d	f	j	i	g	r
p	q	e	m	n	s	a
i	p	h	r	b	i	u
g	x	w	a	i	o	t
f	i	g	e	g	g	w
s	r	n	c	p	e	i
u	b	d	i	g	k	g
y	f	e	n	f	q	x

Page 47

119

Answers

Page 48

a	d	z	x	b	f	c
t	y	u	p	e	i	h
i	f	v	i	t	n	s
n	g	j	n	k	r	p
q	l	m	o	e	t	w
w	i	n	y	k	f	h
a	r	v	u	i	b	k
b	i	n	s	n	q	d

Page 53

wet pet, big wig

Page 54

b	c	h	o	r	s	e
g	o	r	e	q	z	w
v	w	i	l	n	o	f
y	p	m	u	d	t	o
g	o	a	t	y	r	x
n	a	p	l	i	o	n
q	u	k	g	c	f	l
m	o	n	k	e	y	i

Page 59

Page 60

p	b	o	o	t	e	s
h	a	t	q	b	c	w
d	r	i	d	k	n	e
s	j	g	d	w	f	a
h	l	a	r	h	o	t
i	u	x	e	y	d	e
r	z	r	s	c	m	r
t	m	i	t	t	e	n

Page 64

w	a	x	r	m	b	e
s	v	z	k	h	i	n
i	y	t	g	e	t	s
t	t	f	i	b	k	u
c	l	q	o	w	d	j
f	i	t	m	l	i	f
v	n	p	u	i	t	e
h	i	t	a	t	c	h

Page 49

Page 55

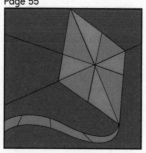

Page 65

Page 50

Page 56

mitten
pants
hat
boot
sweater

Page 61

d	r	e	s	s			p
				o			a
				c			n
				s	k	i	r	t
				h			s
				i			
				r			
	h	a	t				

Page 66

l	o	g	e	h	b	m
x	f	l	y	o	a	c
d	n	k	z	g	r	v
t	b	o	g	s	i	d
q	p	a	j	w	u	o
b	l	v	r	f	t	g
j	o	g	s	o	c	h
e	d	p	y	g	x	i

Page 51

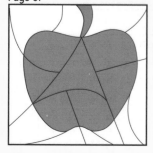

Pages 57

skirt
shirt
socks
shoes
belt

Page 58

1. mitten
2. hat
3. pants
4. sock
5. dress

Page 62

d	o	q	r	i	p	k
i	m	a	w	b	d	r
p	o	n	p	l	u	h
c	u	y	g	i	e	z
h	i	p	v	p	s	i
w	k	u	q	c	g	p
a	p	t	i	p	j	t
r	m	y	b	h	x	e

Page 67

Page 52

Page 63

Page 68

Page 69

Page 70

Page 71

dog jog, pig jig

Page 72

Page 73

- bet, jet, set, pet, get, wet, net
- bin, fin, win, pin, tin
- fog, log, dog, jog, hog, bog
- tip, lip, dip, hip, sip, rip
- fit, sit, hit, kit, pit, lit

Page 75

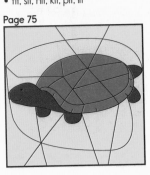

Page 76

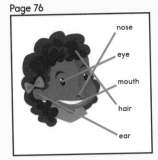

nose
eye
mouth
hair
ear

Page 77

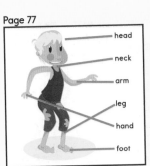

head
neck
arm
leg
hand
foot

Page 78

hand
eye
nose
foot
ear

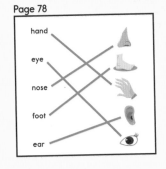

Page 81

e			
a	r	m	
r	o		
	u		
	t		
h	a	n	d
	o		
	s		
e	y	e	

Page 82

e	q	r	b	l	a	s
b	o	p	f	d	m	u
c	j	n	t	o	w	x
y	m	o	p	i	g	
k	v	z	l	a	y	h
i	p	t	b	p	e	o
f	h	o	u	o	z	p
r	m	p	b	p	b	k

Page 83

Page 84

a	z	q	c	l	r	k
e	n	b	l	f	o	m
s	o	d	o	u	t	x
f	t	m	t	v	w	p
h	j	u	a	p	i	o
r	c	h	o	t	s	t
y	q	g	f	o	h	l
d	o	t	t	v	f	a

Page 85

Page 86

a	e	z	x	d	b	h
r	y	u	t	e	o	c
r	o	f	r	n	w	p
w	g	v	o	j	k	w
i	l	m	h	e	t	s
m	o	w	y	l	f	h
a	r	v	u	o	b	k
t	n	i	s	w	q	

Page 87

Page 88

Page 89

Page 90

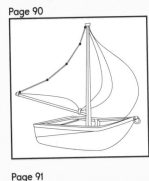

Page 91

hot pot, bow row

Page 92

g	h	e	a	d	l	n
b	c	z	x	i	p	o
n	e	c	k	q	r	s
a	v	m	b	u	w	e
l	n	f	o	o	t	k
e	f	e	s	j	p	
g	q	t	d	i	v	b
a	k	o	e	a	r	n

Page 93

Answers

Page 94

Page 95
1. egg
2. apple
3. ham
4. banana
5. cake

Page 96

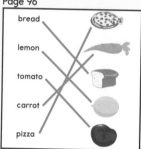

bread
lemon
tomato
carrot
pizza

Page 99

h	a	m		
p				b
p	i	z	z	a
l				n
e	g	g		a
				n
		c	a	k	e

Page 100

a	l	t	t	u	b	k
s	p	e	b	m	o	q
j	s	u	b	c	h	i
g	v	d	w	f	z	r
u	c	r	x	k	i	u
c	o	h	u	b	y	b
u	a	l	v	d	x	e
b	d	n	r	z	u	f

Page 101

Page 102

c	f	m	o	x	d	p
b	e	n	h	i	u	w
u	h	i	u	t	g	q
g	a	l	g	d	w	p
k	n	v	i	r	u	z
r	u	g	a	m	u	l
e	d	s	x	u	q	g
t	u	g	z	g	e	h

Page 103

Page 104

b	u	n	g	i	r	t
a	h	u	y	k	f	n
c	d	x	l	o	u	s
d	p	l	y	w	n	z
m	u	y	n	e	v	p
t	n	r	f	l	r	f
s	u	n	h	i	u	x
z	a	d	i	n	n	e

Page 105

Page 106

a	z	q	y	c	i	t
s	l	p	v	u	k	w
r	u	t	o	t	r	n
b	f	m	h	e	x	g
t	g	d	k	v	i	u
o	l	n	s	h	z	t
n	u	t	q	u	e	r
y	w	a	m		b	u

Page 107

Page 108
cub sub, bug tug

Page 109

Page 110

Page 111
sun fun, cut nut

Page 112

over
under
front
back

Page 113

Page 114

Page 115

b	a	c	k	a	f	s
e	q	r	b	m	r	u
z	u	l	t	w	o	x
y	n	o	p	g	n	h
k	d	z	l	y	t	i
i	e	t	b	p	e	p
s	r			o	v	e	r
r	m	p	c	l	k	d

Page 116

c	a	r	r	o	t
a				r	
k			h	a	n	d
e				n	
		l	e	g	
			e	a	r

Page 117
1. sun
2. rug
3. bow
4. pot
5. top